BY CR

with A

SEE
– THROUGH –
LIFE

WHAT HAPPENS WHEN GUYS
**GET REAL, GET HONEST,
GET ACCOUNTABLE**

YouthMinistry.com/TOGETHER

See-Through Life:
What Happens When Guys Get Real, Get Honest, Get Accountable

Copyright © 2014 Craig Gross and Adam Palmer

group.com
simplyyouthministry.com

Credits
Authors: Craig Gross and Adam Palmer
Executive Developer: Jason Ostrander
Chief Creative Officer: Joani Schultz
Editor: Rob Cunningham
Copy Editor: Stephanie Martin
Art Director: Veronica Preston
Production Artist: Brian Fuglestad
Project Manager: Stephanie Krajec

ISBN 978-1-4707-1247-1

10 9 8 7 6 5 4 3 2 1   20 19 18 17 16 15 14

Printed in the United States of America.

TABLE OF CONTENTS

PART 1:
FLIP THE SWITCH

(AKA, BEING OPEN IS A GOOD THING)

The world you're growing up in looks pretty different from the one I did. When I was your age—which, honestly, wasn't all that long ago—it was possible to do something really stupid (and by "stupid" I mean, like, "over-the-top, beyond-your-dreams dumb") and not have it affect your future too much. Sure, your parents would probably find out about it, and you'd get in serious trouble at home. You'd probably get grounded for a time, lose your TV or Internet privileges, or have your car taken away from you, but rarely would you have to worry about some poor decision-making skills on your part destroying your entire world and making the global population hate you.

> In case you didn't know this already:
> Those days are gone.
>
> An even more sobering thought:
> They aren't coming back.

This is a different world now, and it seems to be changing ever more rapidly the longer we're around. Thanks to the Internet, along with humanity's collective ability to carry a powerful and technologically innovative computer/camera/communication device around in a pocket at all times, your world is under more scrutiny today than ever before. All the instant connectivity at your fingertips, combined with the ability to share just about anything on a whim through social media, means you have to be more careful about what you say and do than any generation before you.

These days, you just can't afford to do something dumb and have it plastered all over the Internet. Countless lives have been ruined, careers shipwrecked, trajectories altered, and futures abandoned because some teenager made a bad spur-of-the-moment choice and got in trouble either with the law or a social network.

In other words, the world you're living in is already open—much more than ever before.

> So you have to live smart.

> You have to embrace being open.

> You have to *live* open.

What do I mean by that phrase, that you should be "living open"? Well, I sure don't mean you need to reflexively blare everything you do, feel, see, and eat through every social media platform you have an account with. I don't mean you constantly point your phone's camera at yourself and post your every waking moment through a series of selfies, because selfies can take you only so far.

In fact, what I'm talking about is the opposite of that. I'm not opposed to you having a picture of yourself; I'm just saying it's about time for you to be bringing another person or two into that picture.

I'm talking about making yourself accountable.

I'm talking about inviting one or two close friends into your world to help you live a strong life and achieve the many goals I hope you've set for your life—and so you can return the favor and do the same thing for them.

This is what I mean by living open. About being open. About embracing openness.

Now, before we can talk about being open, we have to make sure that what you hear when I say "be open" and what I mean are the same thing. Because right now, chances are good that they probably aren't. Maybe you, like a lot of people—if not most people—automatically think of something like "accountability" as a bad thing, like your parents holding you accountable by looking over your shoulder while you do homework or text your friends. This actually isn't the case! In fact, it isn't what I mean at all.

This might blow your mind, but it's true: Accountability is actually a *good* thing.

Let me repeat that, because it's important that you get it. And just to make sure you fully absorb this truth, I'm going to put it on a line all by itself:

Accountability. Is. A. Good. Thing.

One more time, just to make sure, and I'll make it even simpler. Tweet-sized:

ACCOUNTABILITY = GOOD

Now it's your turn. Fill in the blank:

ACCOUNTABILITY = _____

The more I've traveled and spoken about this idea of living an open life full of accountability, the more I've noticed that people automatically turn up their noses at just the idea of making themselves accountable to others. Mainly that's because when we hear phrases like "keep people accountable," they're inevitably tied to news stories about some CEO or investment banker or politician who did something illegal and now must be brought to justice or made to pay for the innocent, unsuspecting lives they ruined.

With those images in mind, we tend to think of accountability as some form of punishment, instead of what it actually is: a life-giving boundary, a necessity in the modern world, a survivalist's backpack filled with a GPS unit, a box of Clif Bars, and a packet of waterproof matches that will keep you alive in the wilderness that is life.

So the very first step you must take to becoming open is to flip the switch that resides in your brain. You need to reframe this topic in your mind and start thinking about accountability in its true, positive light instead of the negative one that automatically springs to mind.

Being open isn't about restraining you or preventing you from doing something bad. It's about helping you do something good.

In fact, let's pause for a moment. Take a second to write down three things you think are good, and then write down a way that being open can be like each of those things.

3 THINGS THAT ARE GOOD

-
-
-

HOW IS BEING OPEN
LIKE THOSE 3 THINGS?

OK, so it probably isn't enough for me to just tell you that accountability is a good thing; I'm guessing you're interested in learning *how* it's good. I'm glad you brought that up! With that in mind, let's take a brief look at four ways being open is a good thing. Those four things are:

- Being open provides safety.

- Being open leads to depth.

- Being open allows freedom and liberty.

- Being open is necessary.

Got 'em? Great. Now that we have an overview, let's look at each one more in depth.

CHAPTER 1

BEING OPEN PROVIDES SAFETY

First off, let's define the kind of safety we're talking about here, because there are two different kinds. There's the smart, wise kind of safety—like buckling your seat belt when you get in the car or putting a protective case on your smartphone—and then there's the more reactionary, fear-based kind of safety—like never driving anywhere or having only a landline.

I'm talking about the first kind.

To me, the concept of safety has nothing to do with curling up under the covers and refusing to interact with the world at large. Nor does it have anything to do with keeping your mouth shut at all times so you don't unintentionally say something that might possibly make someone mad (though this might be a good strategy at times).

When I'm talking about the safety that accountability provides, I'm talking about the kind that sets you up with confidence so you can enjoy life to the fullest. This is the safety you feel just before you get strapped into a roller coaster: the comfort that helps you relax and enjoy the thrill of the ride because you know you're going to make it to the end all right.

We've all seen those movies or TV shows where a lost party of people is forced to wander through some mysterious wilderness or thick jungle trying to find an ancient or magical artifact, or trying to make it back to civilization. Inevitably, our heroes make their way through the dense foliage until they come to a rickety suspension bridge. You know the kind I'm talking about: the bridge made up of just a few ropes and some moldy wooden boards that somehow stretch across a scary-high drop (a drop that usually ends in a rushing river or pile of sharp rocks). Someone from the group will always test it out first, someone else in the traveling party will assure them it's safe, and then, when the person gets halfway across, a board will always break out from underneath their feet and fall down, down, down, taking forever to reach the bottom. Meanwhile, our hero looks on with wide eyes and held breath. Does the same fate await them?!?

Now, compare that kind of nerve-rattling, literally shaky experience from the world of fictional movies and TV shows to the types of bridges we actually experience in the regular world. From highway overpasses to interstate bridges to pedestrian footways in public parks, our world is full of bridges that we cross and *never think about.* That's how secure they are. That's how confident we are that these bridges will support us and carry us on our way without incident.

You may have heard about a 2013 incident from Washington state, when a semi truck carrying an oversized load of drilling equipment was traveling on Interstate 5, crossing the Skagit River on a bridge that had been recently inspected. Unfortunately, the truck driver accidentally made contact with the outside trusses that supported the bridge, causing a portion to collapse and plunge into the river below. Thankfully, no one was killed in the incident, though three people sustained injuries after falling into the river. The bridge was closed for about a month, disrupting the local economy and transit through that region.

The reason you may remember this incident is because it was news. Why was it news? Because bridge collapses in the United States—especially on well-traveled roads and interstate highways—are so incredibly rare. That's how much we've come to depend on them and how much confidence we have in them. We don't cross our fingers whenever we drive on an overpass. We don't even pause before crossing to check it out with a cautious toe. We just keep doing whatever we were doing.

The rickety suspension bridge that always gives way in the movies? That's a life without accountability.

The actual kind, the bridge with failures so rare that they're news? That's a picture of the safety provided by being open.

Accountability gives you unflinching safety and support, the kind of safety that lets you journey through life knowing that someone you love is backing you up, no matter what—and that you're doing the same thing for that person. No comfort compares to this kind of safety.

Now it's your turn. List five ways you can see accountability providing safety in your life:

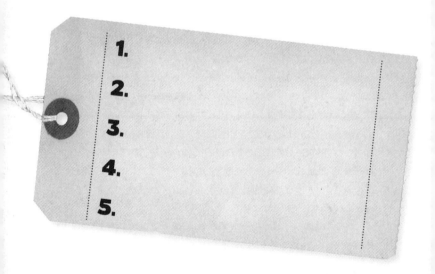

1.

2.

3.

4.

5.

CHAPTER 2

BEING OPEN LEADS TO DEPTH

Have you ever been so into something—say, a book series, a TV show, some hilarious social media account, a sports team, a certain fashion brand, or whatever—that you had to go deep into it? You stayed up late several nights in a row inhaling the next volume in the trilogy or stuck in front of a screen thinking, *I should really go to bed, but...just one more episode.* Or maybe you've already planned out how you'll spend a large chunk of your next paycheck on a specific brand of shoes, or you're saving up for whatever product that tech company thinks up next.

The point is that most of us, if not all of us, like to go deep. In fact, I can't think of anyone in my world, even among my acquaintances, who is shallow and proud of it. Yes, we all have areas where we don't know a whole lot. In fact, most of our knowledge is of this type. There's a lot that we kind of know, a whole lot more that we don't know at all, and then a little bit that we know *a lot about.*

That's depth.

Whatever interests you, that's what you go deep into. It's just a natural part of our human curiosity to want to know more—that's the way we grow and contribute to our culture and society.

But there's one thing all of us tend not to know very well, and some of us are actively opposed to going deep on that thing. What's that one thing?

Ourselves.

Sometimes we're too scared to learn more about ourselves, and other times we just lack the resources to really dig deep into our own hearts and minds to discover who we *really* are and what *actually* makes us tick.

That's where accountability comes in. By putting accountability to work for you, by learning to be open with a select few people you invite into your world, you're able to focus on the task—sometimes difficult, sometimes pleasant—of deepening yourself.

One of the most deepening things about being open is the way you're able to draw each other out through the questions and conversations you'll inevitably have. This act of taking time and being intentional gives you the perfect opportunity to examine yourself and figure out who you *really* are underneath all the unnecessary stuff that life seems to pile on you.

Want to know a really cool thing about going deep? Once you're down there, you'll discover things you never even knew existed. It's like the deep sea, the part of the ocean that's so far down that sunlight can't get to it, making it completely dark. If you can go that deep, you'll uncover many different species of animals that boggle the mind, such as the cookiecutter shark, so named because instead of biting things and tearing them apart, it gouges out round plugs of flesh from its prey; or the lanternfish, a bioluminescent creature whose body glows in the dark; or the flashlight fish, so named because its eyes light up (organs underneath their eyes are actually filled with luminous bacteria, if you can believe it); or the anglerfish, that terrifying fish from *Finding Nemo* that's pretty much all teeth and has a lit-up ball hanging from its head. If you ever want some fuel for nightmare, just search the Internet for pictures of deep-sea fish, and you'll find plenty.

The point, though, isn't to give you a lesson in marine biology. What I'm getting at is this: There are things about yourself that you're nowhere close to knowing yet. Some of them can be fascinating, and more than a few are a bit scary—almost as scary as that anglerfish. But regardless, if you're going to truly live the life God wants for you, then you'll eventually have to learn those things about yourself and learn how to live alongside them.

And that's where going deep can give you the boost you need. By going deep, you get to pull these things up to the surface and really turn them over, examine them, and learn about them—and, by extension, learn about yourself. Pretty cool, huh?

You're in a stage of life right now that is, honestly, all about discovery, about navigating the space between childhood and adulthood, and figuring out what to do with yourself in the meantime. You aren't a kid anymore, but you're also not a full-on, responsible adult yet. Going deep through accountability is a marvelous tool to help you through this.

Additionally, being open deepens your faith. How so? I give you Proverbs 27:17—*As iron sharpens iron, so one person sharpens another.* If you want to sharpen something, you won't get far by, say, waving it around in the air or dragging it along a gravel driveway. No, to sharpen iron, you have to use more iron. The interaction between the two might create a little bit of friction, but it also will result in a sharper edge.

In much the same way, by making yourself accountable in every aspect of your life, including your faith, you're stepping onto an elevator that will take you as deep as you want to go into your beliefs—and into yourself.

Now it's your turn. Write down five areas of your life where you want to go deep:

1.

2.

3.

4.

5.

CHAPTER 3

BEING OPEN ALLOWS FREEDOM AND LIBERTY

So many people view accountability as being "sin management," a bunch of rules and regulations that define all the stuff you're doing wrong. You have your list of all the ways you can fail, and then you catalog those failures so you can puke them up during your accountability-group meeting, feel ashamed, get barked at, and then leave feeling worse than before, knowing you're about to go back out into the world and return to not measuring up.

Please don't do this.

That's not what I'm talking about *at all*.

One problem with this approach is that it puts all the emphasis on your own efforts. *You* bear all the weight for all your slip-ups and mistakes, which isn't a support structure by any means.

The other problem with assuming that being open is basically like "sin management" is that it puts your vision entirely on what you're trying *not* to do, shifting you into a negative mentality and approach to your behavior. It's like flipping a visor down in front of your face (or Google Glass, if that makes it easier to picture—do an online search for Google Glass if you have no idea what I'm talking about) that fills your total field of vision with a giant, blinking sign that constantly screams at you, "DON'T DO IT!!!"

Instead of minimizing the things, thoughts, and behaviors in your world that you want to avoid, this approach essentially blows them up until they're the only things you can see. This makes them appear all the more inescapable and inevitable.

But there's good news here! When you approach accountability with the proper mindset—that it's good and beneficial—then being open frees you up to do the helpful things you want to do, to think the pure thoughts you want to think, to practice the positive behaviors you want to incorporate into your lifestyle.

That's the whole point of accountability, anyway: to feel free to achieve some goal or goals that make your life better. Think about it: Which would make your time at school better, focusing on the fact that you're getting an education that will serve you all your life or focusing on an intense desire to not fail each of your classes? Which point of view would send you running into school every morning with hope, and which would send you trudging in with a sense of nearly unbearable dread?

When you're accountable, you pay attention to the positivity in your world and walk with freedom and liberty. Instead of looking over your shoulder, worrying that you're about to get cuffed and arrested by the Sin Police, you can walk through life with your head held high and your eyes locked on the goals that lie on the horizon.

Are you starting to get a vision for the types of freedom and liberty you can have? Write them down here:

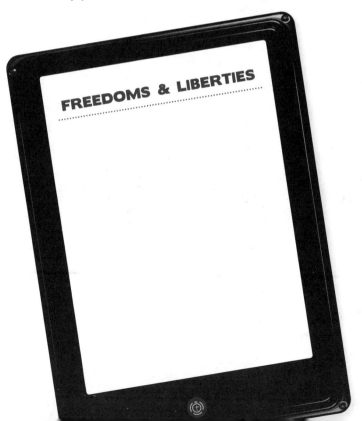

FREEDOMS & LIBERTIES

CHAPTER 4

BEING OPEN IS NECESSARY

Here's the thing about secrets: They almost always come out, and trying to keep them can drive us crazy. We instinctively know this, especially when we're contemplating doing something we know is wrong and start trying to convince ourselves it's really OK because "No ever needs to know about it."

Come on, you know you've told yourself this before. You can admit it. We're being open here.

The second we start thinking we can keep a secret is the second we have proof that being open is necessary.

Now, please understand that I'm not talking about harmless or helpful secrets. If you know a surprise birthday party is in the works for a friend, or if someone's confided something to you that they'd rather the whole world not know about, then you can hang on to those secrets. In the first case, it will come out eventually when your friend walks into a darkened room and everyone shouts, "Surprise!" In the other case, something you're told in confidence as a means of finding healing isn't so much a secret as private information not meant for public consumption. (I'm assuming, of course, you weren't told something that's illegal or that results in the person being hurt; if they're in danger or doing something unlawful, you need to talk about it with an authority figure you trust.)

No, I'm talking about the types of secrets that lead to a downfall. Pro golfer Tiger Woods, former Congressman Anthony Weiner, Toronto Mayor Rob Ford—when their secrets came out, those guys went from being great at what they do to becoming a punch line.

The problem with secrets is that they grow larger and heavier until they eventually pull us under and become our undoing. That's why being open is so necessary— because when we're open, instead of keeping those secrets to ourselves, we can share them with one another, just as the Apostle Paul encourages us to do in Galatians 6:2—*Carry each other's burdens, and in this way you will fulfill the law of Christ.*

When we carry each other's baggage through accountability, we're spreading the weight around to many different hands and enabling each of us to walk upright and proud. Plus, if the second half of this verse is to be believed, then when we help each other this way, we're doing God's work. Plain and simple.

You know, I first started learning about being open when I was your age. Just after I'd completed my sophomore year, my youth pastor at the time, a guy named Tom, asked if I'd be interested in meeting with him one-on-one at a local McDonald's one morning each week. I wasn't sure I could handle the early-morning time at first, but the more I thought about it, the more I realized how great it could be.

I've always been a pretty outgoing, confident guy. One reason I've been able to build a career as a speaker and minister is because of my natural abilities to connect with just about anyone. The only problem is that if you're this kind of person with those types of abilities, you can reach a place where you have a lot of acquaintances but not many deep friendships. I had a lot of the former and none of the latter. Tom offered me a lifeline when he reached out to me, so I took it.

In fact, as I pondered this even further, I began to see how good being open could be. I lacked not only a person or people in my life who I could go deep with, but I also lacked the capability to go deep. I didn't know how to do it or even how to go about it. Tom was offering me the chance to have both: the skill set to go deep and the person to go deep with.

Tom and I started meeting, and it was great. I hadn't even known how beneficial being open would be for me until I started doing it. And once it began, I knew I would keep this a part of my life for as long as I drew breath on this earth. I finally had someone I could get real with: I could talk about my faith, my doubts and struggles, my fears about the past and my hopes for the future. I could talk about my temptations and the things I wrestled with on a regular basis. I could talk about anything and everything—and no matter what I said, it was OK.

So much safety. So much freedom. So much weight lifted off my shoulders, and all because I decided to take someone up on his offer to get open.

But here's the great thing, and the point I want to make: In addition to finding freedom and liberty by unburdening myself, I also had the wonderful opportunity to learn how to listen to someone else as they did that very same thing. That's because Tom used this opportunity to teach me about true openness and shared some of his own challenges. Now, he made sure that everything he mentioned was age-appropriate, and he didn't try to unload his adult responsibilities onto someone who was still a kid. I wasn't Tom's sole accountability partner; I was just one of many high school students to whom he was teaching a valuable life skill. He opened up himself and showed me just a part of his inner world. And by doing so, he taught me how to listen and be trustworthy, how to care for something as valuable as another person's thoughts and feelings.

Tom and I met like this for about a year, until he suggested the following summer that we welcome my good friend Jake into our weekly meetings and go from being a sort of mentor relationship into something that more closely resembled an accountability group. I thought it sounded like a great idea, so I floated it to Jake. He agreed with me that it was something we could both use, so we started meeting regularly with Tom during our senior year in high school.

It was great. All the things in this book, all the practical advice and tools I give out when I talk about accountability—all that stuff got its start in those meetings with Tom, Jake, and me.

Tom taught us the overwhelming truth that accountability is good.

He taught us how we should go about keeping one another accountable.

He taught us the ins and outs of being open, being honest, and being real.

He taught us that the whole point of being open wasn't to sit across from someone and be their judge but to sit beside them and be their advocate.

Tom taught us that being open is all about talking

and listening, with both things working in concert to create a web of support that helps us carry one another's burdens.

Want to have a full and satisfying life now, through the rest of your school years, and well into adulthood? Then you need to get accountable.

You need to get open.

So what's it take to do that? Let's look a little more closely at the practical things you'll need to start living open.

YOUR TURN

Here are a few things that might prevent you from getting open. Circle the three you most respond to:

- Too vulnerable

- Too honest

- Fear of rejection

- Don't want to change

- Don't feel the need to change

- Happy with where I am

- Too busy

- Too hard

- Too much work

- No one to do it with

- I don't see my reason on this list; here it is:

  _____

Now look at the three things you've circled and write down the reasons they're lame excuses:

1.

2.

3.

PART 2:
THE TO-DO LIST

(AKA, WHAT DOES IT TAKE TO BE OPEN?)

OK, I hope that by now we've established that being open and staying that way is a good, healthy, honest, and positive thing for you. But now that you're convinced to try out accountability, you're probably starting to think up more than just a few questions about what to do next. Questions such as:

- What sort of roads will I have to travel to get open?

- What sort of practical benefits will I see from traveling those roads?

- Are those two things somehow linked together?

Let's start by answering that first question, and once we figure it out, I think you'll have the answers to the other two.

Accountability has three basic components, three attributes it requires in order to work, and they aren't necessarily what you'd expect. Those three things are honesty, courage, and community, and they work kind of like milestones on a road. If you don't embrace these three things, you'll just be spinning your wheels. Let's examine them more closely, and you'll see why.

CHAPTER 5

IT TAKES HONESTY

We've all been to the produce section of the grocery store, that magical, colorful place where everything is sold by the pound and you get to pick the amount you want. Maybe your mom sometimes asks you to run into the store and pick up a few things she forgot. Because most of us don't pick our own apples from a tree or grapes from a vine, it's kind of neat to select the items you want and put them on the scales in the produce section. That way you know how much you have and can figure out how much it'll cost to buy that plastic bag full of Granny Smith apples.

Then there's the deli, where you can ask the person behind the counter for a pound-and-a-half of roasted turkey, and they have a handy scale to measure it. Except this time it's usually just a flat plate with a digital readout and a label maker. They'll measure your pound-and-a-half of roasted turkey, push a button to spit out the label with a bar code and price, wrap up the meat, slap that label on there, and hand it over so you can go pay for it.

Scales have been a crucial component in the world of markets for a long time, though they haven't always been spring-loaded or digital. For centuries, the market scale was the "balance" type. You probably know what I'm talking about: two saucers suspended by chains from a single beam with a pivot in the center. Shopkeepers had a set of weights, so you'd order a pound of whatever you wanted and they'd place their single-pound weight on one side. Then they'd measure the thing you were buying on the other side until the scale balanced out. One pound on each side, right?

Except, not always. It became very common for merchants to shave down their weights by just a fraction so their single-pound weight became really, say, 15 ounces (in case you don't remember, there are 16 ounces in a pound). That enabled them to sell slightly less stuff for more money. Sure, they'd be cheating their customers, but they were willing to do that, especially because *everyone else* was doing it.

A couple of London merchants knew this practice was going on—in fact, everyone knew it—and decided to be open and live honestly. They got together and started checking out each other's scales. One week one of them would verify the honesty of the other guy's scales, and then the following week they'd switch roles.

Word spread about these independently verified and trustworthy scales, so customers started taking their business to these merchants. When all the other merchants started losing business to the honest guys, they suddenly decided that honesty was the best policy. So they got in on the action, banding together with the original honest guys to form a trade association called (and this is real) the Most Worshipful Company of Livery Merchants.

This association began having a wider-reaching impact on even non-grocery merchants. Eventually they wound up influencing the British government to create an official department to oversee standardized measurements—a department that still exists today.

Kinda crazy how far a little honesty can go, isn't it?

The cool thing about honesty is that it really does cut through the nonsense like a bright ray of sunshine. Another cool thing about honesty is that it is, by definition, impossible to fake.

And if you try to fake your way through being open, you won't go far.

In fact, if you aren't prepared to be honest, then what's the point?

There's really no point in attempting accountability if you aren't also going to open yourself to honesty. To own up to the times when you don't behave like a shining star. To be vulnerable to a couple of people you can trust to hear your heart without judgment.

If you're going to hold back or misrepresent yourself in the context of accountability, then you probably shouldn't even mess with it.

But there's another side to this coin of honesty: You have to partner with other people who are committed to being open alongside you and are willing to go completely down the road of honesty with you. You can't be the only vulnerable one, the only open one, the only honest one.

You must bring people into your picture of accountability who are *also* willing to take an unvarnished look in the mirror with you and accept whatever reflection shows up. That means both you and they are willing to not only ask honest questions but also to answer them honestly—and hear those answers honestly.

It can be tough to truly hear people at their most honest and vulnerable. Not only can it make us uncomfortable, but we sometimes don't know how to hear those honest answers *without being judgmental*. That's especially true if a person we love has just admitted to some embarrassing or possibly reprehensible behavior.

Additionally, we also have to be ready to be challenged and disagreed with. We must be honest enough with ourselves to admit that we don't have all the answers, we don't have this world figured out yet, and we might *never* get that way. The last thing you need when you're trying to get and stay open is someone who tells you that everything you're doing is great and you don't need to change or improve anything. And you don't need to be that person, either.

But all these things require honesty. Are you ready to handle that? Because if not, then you might as well just be chatting about the weather.

Now it's your turn to "balance out the scale," just as the Most Worshipful Company of Livery Merchants did. Take a look at the spaces below; on one side write down an area of your life where you could use some honesty, and on the other side write down an honest response to that area.

HONESTY NEEDED

RESPONSE

CHAPTER 6

IT TAKES COURAGE

Another crucial component of the accountability relationship, and one that goes hand in hand with honesty, is courage. Think of honesty as the road map: You want to get from your house to this destination far away, and honesty is the map that'll show you the way there. (Let's face it: No one uses maps anymore, so maybe we should call honesty the directions you got off the Internet or what came up when you typed an address into the Maps app on your smartphone.) But what good is a map if you don't have any way to travel? It isn't enough just to know your destination, or even to have the path to your destination outlined clearly. You must also find something to get you to that destination, because you won't get there with wishes and dreams.

So if honesty is the guide that provides the path that will show you how to get where you want to go, then courage is the vehicle that actually takes you there.

In simple terms: Courage is honesty in action.

A few pages back, we talked about all the aspects of honesty that accountability requires. Well, they all take courage.

Do you have to ask honest questions? You'll need some courage.

Do you have to answer those honest questions, too? Guess what—that will take a little bit of courage as well. Actually, it will take a *whole lot of courage.*

Do you need to hear those answers with advocating honesty that simply listens without passing judgment? That can take some serious courage, too.

One thing about being open is that it provides us with an opportunity to deal with some of the stuff in our world or from our life that scares us—and courage helps us look into those scary places and tackle what we find. Courage helps us deal with the tough stuff in our lives, from past hurts to current habits to future hang-ups. The accountability environment provides us with a safe place to deal with those things; courage provides us with the strength we need.

You'll notice that I'm talking about courage and fear in the same sentence, and perhaps that seems like a mistake to you. After all, if you have courage, doesn't that mean you're no longer afraid of something? Actually, it's quite the opposite! Courage is the boldness to admit you have fears yet are still willing to look them in the eye and face them down. Because the fact is, we all have fears. We all have scary stuff in our closets that we'd rather not talk about or deal with.

Honesty lets you admit those fears; courage gives you the club for smacking them in the face. Courage is what lets you march confidently into battle, trusting that God will give you the strength to face your fears and that he'll be trustworthy in helping you conquer them. Especially because you know you aren't going to face them alone—you have your accountability partner(s) marching in there, right alongside you, ready to help you however they can.

That's what I mean when I talk about courage.

Now it's your turn. Think of the arrow below as a map; write your goals on the far end—that's your destination. In what areas of your life will you need to be courageous in order to reach that destination? Write those above the arrow.

CHAPTER 7

IT TAKES COMMUNITY

I have many friends, but a couple of my best friends are two guys named Ryan and Jake. They're the kind of people I would go to the mat for in any situation, because I know they'd do the same for me. When I get in a jam and don't know what to do, these are the people (besides my wife) who I immediately think to call.

One thing I love about Ryan and Jake is how intense they are, how driven they are to make themselves better, both on their own and also when they get together. Ryan and Jake are both workout enthusiasts, if not necessarily healthy-living enthusiasts. They love to work out, to stretch their bodies to the breaking point, and they actually think grueling things such as long bike rides and marathons are fun.

Anyway, Ryan and Jake were training for a triathlon (a two-and-a-half mile swim, followed by a 112-mile bike ride, followed by a little thing known as a marathon, which is running for 26.2 miles) and were really whipping themselves into shape. They don't live in the same city, so they were training with separate groups of people, athletes who could help them get better and better until they were in the kind of shape to perform in a triathlon and not die.

Amid this season of training, Ryan and Jake both had to come to a meeting in Southern California, where I live, so while they were together, they decided to go out one morning for a training run of 13 miles.

For fun.

These guys are my friends, but I don't always understand them.

Anyway, Ryan and Jake met up, stretched out, and did all the other stuff you have to do to prepare yourself mentally and physically for a 13-mile run. And just before they were about to start, they got into a conversation about the pace at which they'd run. For all you non-runners, when you're covering a distance like that, you try to keep a certain pace going, like a rhythm you can get into that helps you go the distance.

Jake, who was the strongest person in his training group back home, was confident he could maintain any pace Ryan wanted to run. Meanwhile, Ryan, who intentionally trained with people who were stronger and faster than him, figured he could outpace Jake pretty easily. So between the two of them, they decided Ryan could set the pace.

Then they were off. Ryan started at a pace that would have them going about a mile every eight minutes, and

Jake had no problem keeping up—for the first three miles or so.

By the fourth mile—not even a third of the way through their run—Jake began feeling the difficulty of the pace and started losing a couple of steps to Ryan. Now, instead of running side by side, Jake was just a few feet behind Ryan but still was managing to keep up. It was hard, but Jake did it—for the next four miles.

Around the eighth mile (if you do the math, you'll realize they'd been running for an hour nonstop at this point—I'm exhausted just typing that out), Ryan was still in his comfort zone while Jake was doing some serious work just to maintain forward motion.

So Ryan decided he'd kick it up to the next level and knock about 30 seconds off the pace to make it a mile every seven-and-a-half minutes. Amazingly, though Jake lost another couple of steps and fell another few feet behind Ryan, he still managed to keep up. He was in complete agony, but he was there.

Three miles later, around mile 11 or so (roughly 90 minutes into their run), Ryan began feeling the burn of his natural limits, but he was determined to keep this quicker pace going, especially because Jake was still hanging on his heels. Plus, they had only two miles left, and Ryan wanted to finish strong.

But so did Jake. The last two miles were uphill, which made their desire to push themselves even greater. Neither runner wanted to let up, so although they were both getting winded by that point, they kept going and going and going. Running uphill is hard already; running uphill when all you've been doing for the last hour-and-a-half is running and all you want to do is beat the other guy but he won't slow down to let you—well, that's something else. That's Olympic-level dedication.

Both Ryan and Jake gutted out those last two miles until they finally got back to where they started, crossing the predetermined finish line in triumph. Jake fell to the ground in a very ungraceful manner, grateful to be done, while Ryan sort of crouched down and did his best to breathe and give himself a rest.

This is a wonderful illustration of the power of community, the great things that can happen when we welcome others into our world and give them the go-ahead to challenge us in what we do. Neither Jake nor Ryan, running on his own, would ever have been able to keep up that pace. But because they were together, encouraging each other, spurring each other on through healthy competition toward a clear-cut goal, they found deeper reserves of strength and determination within them than they probably knew existed.

One thing we as people have seen time and again, both in the Bible and throughout history, is that it's extremely difficult to do anything worth doing by yourself. The Bible is packed with people who had help getting things done, even from the very beginning. God looked at Adam and said, basically, "This guy shouldn't be alone. I'll make someone to help him out."

Yes, a few people in the Bible accomplished some incredible feats solo, but you'll notice that they generally didn't *continue* doing stuff on their own. David defeated Goliath by himself (well, God had a *little* something to do with it), but that's the only battle recorded in the Bible where David did his own thing. From then on, he had either an army or his "mighty men" to back him up.

Here's an interesting side note, as long as we're on the subject: David, by being off doing his own thing alone on his palace rooftop, put himself in a position to be tempted to sin with Bathsheba. (Check out the story in 2 Samuel 11.) It's because he was alone—instead of out with his army, where he should've been—that he thought he could sleep with someone else's wife and get away with it. It's quite the understatement to say David could've used some accountability that day!

Scan through your history books and you'll see person after person who had some help making the world a better place. Why? Because life wasn't meant to be done solo. You need community to live a full life, and you need community to get open.

But community doesn't just fall out of the sky and hit you on the head. You won't wake up one morning and find community sitting on your front lawn with a hot mug of coffee. If you don't already have the types of friends and relationships in your world that you can transform into something for accountability, then you'll have to find them. (We'll discuss this in more depth in the next part of this book.)

The long and the short of it is this: We all need each other, and we need every part of the people we're being open with—the good parts, the bad parts, and everything in between. The truth is, we can do more together, go further together, climb higher together, go deeper together than we ever could alone.

Honesty, courage, and community. You absolutely must have those three things in your world if you're going to get open.

YOUR TURN

Take a few moments to think about honesty, courage, and community. Which of these three things will be the easiest part of being open for you? Which will be the most difficult? Write down your reasons in the spaces below.

1.

2.

3.

PART 3:
RUBBER
MEETS ROAD

(AKA, SO HOW DO I DO IT?)

OK, here we are. We know accountability is a good thing, we know we need to be open, and we know what it takes to be open. So now we just have to figure out how to put all those things together into some practical whole that makes sense within the context of our real world.

First, let me reiterate: Being open isn't just about *talking;* it's also about *listening.* If you're interested in doing accountability so you can have a weekly one-sided conversation about yourself, you won't get far before you start burning through accountability partners.

And when it comes to those partners, it's helpful to remember that the concept of accountability works best with just a few people—seriously, like two or three—who you're in close community with. These people aren't going to be your only friends; you're welcome to have as many friends and acquaintances as your schedule and skills allow, but you can't have an open invitation to your accountability group. It works best when it's small and nimble.

When you decide to get open, when you truly determine to use honesty, courage, and community to get accountable, you're making a decision to go into this all the way, with no half-heartedness. You must be intentional about accountability or it won't work, and you'll wind up spinning your wheels and doing the same things you've been doing.

You'll keep looking at porn instead of looking past it to see God's ideas of healthy sexuality.

You'll keep buying into cultural assumptions that "manhood" is about swagger and external image instead of about the state of your heart and its surrender to Christ.

You'll keep listening to the lie that sex is harmless, consequence-free fun instead of a sacred, soul-bonding act of worship intended for marriage.

You'll keep masturbating instead of mastering your lust.

You'll keep imploding due to stress instead of seeking God's peace and wisdom.

You'll keep wallowing in depression instead of seeking help and walking in the light of Christ.

You'll keep bumping against your family members instead of acting toward them with the same charity and grace you want to receive.

You'll keep wasting money on stupid stuff instead of taking care of the resources God has given you.

You'll keep wandering aimlessly toward your future instead of finding confidence in seeking the guidance of the Lord and the wisdom of others.

You'll keep wondering who you are instead of maximizing your strengths and becoming more acceptable of your weaknesses.

You'll keep believing that "success" has something to do with status and money instead of pursuing the wonderful things that have value in God's kingdom.

You'll keep thinking that education is about cramming and memorizing rather than about gaining the skills you need for an enriching lifetime of learning.

Sound good? Then let's take a look at the nuts and bolts of both getting and maintaining accountability. After all, it's one thing to decide you're going to get open, and it's another thing entirely to keep it going for any lengthy time period. We'll also break down the ways you can get involved in one another's world so you not only get open and stay open but so you also make your accountability effective over the long run.

CHAPTER 8

WHAT ARE YOU LOOKING FOR?

First, let's talk about some traits you'll want to look for in the people you pursue accountability alongside. That will help you figure out who exactly you're going to want to be open with. You'll be making lists in this next section, and as you do so, my hope is that one or two great candidates will rise to the top.

Before you move on, stop and say a prayer that God will bring the best people to your mind as you work through this exercise. This type of endeavor *definitely* needs to be undertaken prayerfully.

GENDER

This trait kind of goes without saying, but I'll say it anyway: You really should be in an accountability relationship with other guys. The types of things you're going to be talking about (check out the list of questions toward the end of this part of the book, if you want an early glimpse of what I mean) aren't something you'd generally be comfortable airing in front of *anyone, let alone someone of the opposite sex.*

No, because you're a guy, being open definitely needs to happen in an environment that is for guys and by guys. Girls are great, and you can have a wonderful relationship with them and all that, but you need to reserve this space just for your fellow men.

Take a minute to list some guys who you might consider welcoming into accountability with you. List as few or as many as you'd like.

ACCOUNTABILITY

BACKGROUND

What's your background like? Are you an athlete? musician? bookworm? Do you come from a large family or a small one? Do you live in the country, the suburbs, or the city? Have you spent your whole life in church, or are you fairly new to the experience? Do you have a history of addiction, or have you kept yourself fairly clean?

These are just a few of the life events and character traits you possess that make up your background. They've contributed to the person you've become, and while no one has the *exact* same background you do, more than a few people in your world have some— if not many—similarities to yours.

Those people whose background is along the same lines as yours, whose history reads very much like yours reads—they are the kinds of people you want to be in accountability with. Why? Because when things start to get real, they'll be more likely to understand where you're coming from, and vice versa. On the next page, list some guys who have a background similar to yours:

SIMILAR BACKGROUND

POINT OF VIEW

By your point of view, I'm talking about the way you see the world. This includes your opinions and preferences, from politics to theology to favorite sports, teams, music, and movies. All that kind of stuff.

So when you're looking for someone to get accountable with, you'll want to find someone with a similar point of view to yours. Notice I didn't say the *exact* same point of view, but *similar*. There's a reason for that.

The way we grow as people is to have our ideas and preconceived notions challenged by outside viewpoints. *So* although it's good to have someone in your corner who can understand where you're coming from and who can champion you in what you believe and think, you also want someone who will push you to grow in ways you wouldn't ordinarily expect.

By forming an accountability relationship with a person or people with a point of view that's similar to yours, you're finding common ground where you guys can relate. At the same time, you're leaving the door open for growth in both directions. You can grow from their input, and they can grow from yours, which is really the point of being open, isn't it?

List some guys who have a similar—but not the exact same—point of view that you do:

SIMILAR POINT OF VIEW

TRUST

When it comes to getting vulnerable and sharing personal stuff, there probably isn't a place where you'll be more vulnerable and get more personal than in your accountability group. Getting open means doing just that: opening up yourself to a few people who will safeguard your secrets.

The only way that plan will work is if you're being open with someone you can trust. Someone you can safely confide in. Someone who'd rather endure a thousand slings and arrows before giving away anything you said during your accountability meeting.

And you have to be the same kind of person.

Having this foundational trust is one of the main things that make being open so great and why it works so well. Because when you sit down with those guys and start getting accountable to one another, it forms a bond like nothing else can.

On the next page, list some guys you know you can trust. If you have any nagging doubts, God might be telling you that they may be decent guys but not be the right ones for such a trust-needing relationship. You want to keep this list to guys you know will be solid:

TRUST

STAGE OF LIFE

By "stage of life," I'm talking about where you are in life, and though I usually mean it in a broader sense (because I usually talk with both men and women of all ages about this topic of being open), it still applies here. If you're a senior at a particular high school, it might not make sense to try to get accountable with a freshman at a different school. Not only is there a wide age gap, but you're also from different stages of life culturally.

That's why it's not a bad idea to invite someone into accountability with you who's roughly in the same stage of life as you and who therefore better understands the types of goals you're hoping to achieve. For example, you and your accountability partner(s) can spur each other toward all that's required to get accepted into college (and get it paid for through scholarships, while you're at it). If you're all graduating the same year, then you can all work together and encourage one another to take all the necessary steps to make that goal happen—and then celebrate together when it does!

On the next page, list some guys who are in the same stage of life as you:

STAGE OF LIFE

So those are the similarities you want to have: *gender, background, point of view, trustworthiness,* and *stage of life.*

Now look at your lists for all those criteria and see how many times you listed the same person. I'm guessing you've written down at least one name in all five lists. If so, that's someone you can get accountable with.

But what if you don't have a clear person after making your lists? That's why you prayed! You can still use the lists to narrow down potential candidates, trusting that God will guide you to the right accountability partner(s).

In either case, whittle the possibilities down until you have two to four people, and then approach them man-to-man (preferably when you're by yourselves) and see if they're interested and willing to be open.

CHAPTER 9

WHAT DOES IT LOOK LIKE?

Now that you have one or two people (or three at the most) to join with you on this adventure to openness, let's get super practical and talk about what your accountability meeting might actually look like. What sort of routine should you have? Where should you meet? What should you *do* when you meet? And how can you set this thing up to have a bit of longevity?

Let's take a look.

ROUTINE

The surest way to watch your accountability group start strong but fizzle out quickly is to be completely random with your meeting days and times, not planning ahead or getting stuff on the schedule, and instead just taking it as it comes and hoping for the best. If you try that approach, I guarantee you'll only wind up frustrated, and your group will be dead within a few months—if it even lasts that long.

You have to treat being open as an important part of your life, which means you need to make room for it. You probably tend to eat on a pretty regular schedule (that is, you likely eat more than once every day), and your classes and extracurricular activities are all on a pretty regular schedule you must follow. Being open is no different.

So even though you may hate schedules and planning and organizing, you have to do it. And it really isn't all that difficult—you just need to carve out an hour or so once a week (or even once every two weeks, though that level of frequency tends to lead to inconsistency because everyone starts to wonder, "Are we meeting this week?").

Get together with the other guys in your group and figure out a weekly time that works for all of you. I know you're busy—we're all busy—but the truth is you make time for things that are important to you. If you can go see a new movie every weekend, you have time for this. If you can devote an entire weekend to marathoning the latest video game, you have time for this. If you find yourself making regular late-night runs to Taco Bell, you have time for this.

So figure out a day and a time that works for everyone, and then put it on the calendar—without fail. Be sure to look ahead, because sometimes holidays and other special occasions can mess with your schedule (especially those like Christmas and the Fourth of July, which happen on a specific date). If you need to schedule around those or make a contingency plan, then do so.

Think through what an entire year will look like for you guys. It would be very easy to start your group at the beginning of summer with the intention of meeting every Friday night—after all, Friday nights in the summer are always free, right?—but then hit a snag when school resumes and suddenly it's football season again, and now Friday nights are game nights. Sure, you can move your meeting time at that point, but if you can choose something now that will work for *most* of the year, then it's all the better for slipping into a routine.

Below is a typical calendar week, from Sunday to Saturday. Write in some possible times when your group can meet.

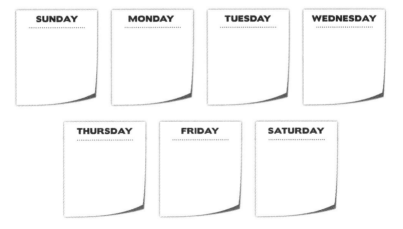

SETTING

Now that you have a day and time, you need to choose a good place to hold your meetings. There's really no objectively perfect place for this; the perfect place for you is, well, wherever you decide to meet. You might want to take a few factors into consideration, however. For starters, an actual physical location is better than trying to meet over the phone or through some sort of video-chat program (though, I must say, those work well if you need them to work for you—my own accountability group consists of people from around the country, so gathering in person weekly poses a major challenge).

When I started getting open, I was in high school just like you, and my friend Jake and I met at McDonald's for about an hour before school once a week. The time we spent together there has led to a lifelong friendship—so much so that we were the best man at each other's weddings, and we're still in an accountability group to this day.

So some place like that works well. You might feel a little more cosmopolitan and decide to go to a neighborhood coffee shop or bakery a little earlier in the morning than you usually wake up. Or you may want to grab lunch together every Saturday afternoon at the same restaurant, or change up the restaurant every week to add some variety.

Some people are comfortable meeting out in public; others aren't. They aren't comfortable with *being* open out *in* the open, and that can make a lot of sense. It can be difficult to talk about your struggles or the things that are holding you back from achieving your goals when other people are in earshot.

This is up to you, but make sure to be considerate of others if you're meeting in public. Be aware that some conversation topics aren't for everyone to hear. If you'll be meeting in a place where you might run into a lot of young kids, for example (like the McDonald's I went to when I was your age, or a public park), you'll want to moderate the tone and volume of your voice so you don't unwittingly expose those kids to ideas and concepts they aren't ready for yet.

You don't have to meet in a public place—they just tend to be the most convenient for people. If you want to meet at someone's house, in their garage or game room or around the kitchen table late at night, that's fine, too. Just find a place where everyone can be themselves and where you know you're safe to say whatever needs to be said.

As I mentioned earlier, if meeting at a physical location isn't possible, then you can turn to technology as an option. This works really well for my group, which uses a free conference-call system, but you can also use video conferencing programs that are generally available for free on most computers, such as Skype or, for you Apple users, iChat AV. Google Plus currently has video "hangouts" that can work really well, too, but you'll need a Google Plus account for that.

Ultimately, it doesn't matter *where you meet*—just make sure you're meeting regularly and taking full advantage of the time you have together.

Take a few moments now to list all the places that might be available for you and your group to meet:

MEETING PLACES

FORMAT

OK, so you've chosen your time and place, and now you're all gathered in the same room with a cup of coffee in hand or are on the same Internet connection with a strong signal and your undivided attention. Now what?

Now it's time to meet!

But what does that look like? What course should your meeting follow? Should there be some sort of itinerary, or should you guys just free-associate and talk about what's going on in your world, mumbling about your struggles and filling any awkward pauses with references to the latest pop-culture event?

I believe you need a plan in place to make accountability worth having. It doesn't have to be a rigid structure, but it does need to be there, and it needs to be fairly consistent from meeting to meeting. Honesty is what you're going for here, and honesty is seldom a random occurrence; honesty springs from the safe confidence of planning.

Here's a short breakdown of what I recommend for your meeting format:

- *Small talk and chitchat.* But only for a couple of minutes—five at the most. You can catch up on your social lives or the movies you've seen *after* the meeting—you're here to hit the ground running.

- *Open with prayer.* Prayer is always a great way to get your mind, heart, and soul focused for the time you have ahead. Ask God to prepare you and make you ready to say what you need to say and hear what you need to hear.

- *Ask the regular general questions.* You'll see a list of these in just a moment, but these are the questions you each ask the other people in the group. In other words, they apply to everyone.

- *Ask the specific questions.* Again, more on this in a moment, but this is when you ask and answer questions that are specific to each particular person.

- *A closing prayer.* Prayer is a great bookend, except this time you're asking God to help you receive the things you heard and to seal those things so that they can have an impact on your daily life as you leave.

- *Any further discussion.* This is when you can resume the small talk or dig more deeply into a concept, thought, or concern that came up during the meeting you just had.

• *Dismiss*. Go your separate ways in peace.

This is just a basic format to get you started. The longer you meet, the more you'll see if this format works for you or if you need to modify it. Please feel free to modify it, as long as you aren't making changes simply to make changes but are indeed making adjustments so it all works better for you.

ASK

Now we've reached the meat of the issue: the questions. As you just read, your meeting will consist mostly of questions being asked and answered by each member of the accountability group. This is your group, so you'll each have some specific things you'll want to get to and unique goals that you're trying to achieve, but before you start in on those questions, I've found that it's good to ask a few general questions to help orient everyone toward the right direction.

Look at the following list of questions and select a few that you think would be good for your group, or have each member pick one or two questions they think should be asked of everyone, making the process all the more democratic. Ideas include:

• How was your week?

- Did the things you said and did this week make your life better? Did they represent you well to the rest of the world?

- How have you treated those who are important to you this week? Did you honor them and treat them with grace and generosity?

- Did you use any of your words as weapons this week, either to someone's face or behind their back?

- What about anger? Are you angry or resentful toward someone? Are you holding on to that anger or letting it go?

- What about your stuff? Have you been trustworthy with your money and belongings this week?

- Have you indulged in lusts or anything of a sexual nature (porn, masturbation, sex of any kind), whether physically or mentally?

- Have you caved in to any of your addictions or weaknesses this week?

- Were you honest and truthful in all you did?

- In one or two words, state how you're feeling emotionally right now.

- If you were triggered and this trigger was new, how can you avoid it in the future?

- State one lie you told someone in the past week, or a secret you're keeping from someone else or this group.

- Did you lie to me/us in your answers to any of these questions?

These questions are just the beginning and are really intended to be conversation starters. If you don't see anything here that relates to what you guys want to do, then by all means use these ideas as a template to figure out your own set of questions that will settle nicely into what your group is all about.

These are the general questions that could work for just about anybody, but they aren't the only questions you'll need to ask. In addition, you'll also have individualized, unique questions that each member of your group will bring to the table.

Whether or not the rest of your group had input on the general questions, this is the part where everyone must have input, because this is where the other guys submit questions about themselves and you submit questions about yourself. In my own group, we just use a couple of those general questions, and then we spend the rest of the time asking each other the specific questions we've created and written ourselves to help us with our specific goals.

To explain, let me give you a hypothetical situation. Let's say you, like me, are seeking accountability so you can get a better handle on your schedule. Of course, we are complex creatures, and I have a lot of good things in my life I need to do, a lot of goals I want to achieve. But a main reason I seek accountability these days is to help me keep a handle on my ever-growing, ever-fluctuating schedule.

So one of the first questions I wrote for myself was about my schedule. When my accountability group meets, someone from my group will ask me: "Craig, did you use your time wisely and productively this week, or were you wasteful?" Think of all the things you want to accomplish at this stage in your life and in the future, and then prioritize them. Which ones are most important to you? Which things do you think would be most beneficial right now, and which can move down on the priority list a bit? Organize your list according to priority, putting your highest-priority goals at the top and lowest-priority goals at the bottom. By "low priority," I don't mean those things are unimportant; in fact, I'm assuming everything on the list will be important to you. I'm just talking about stuff that isn't as much of a priority for you right now, at this stage of your life.

The amazing thing about living a life of accountability is that it helps you grow as a person. Ultimately you'll achieve the goals you want to reach and then move forward to establishing and reaching new goals! The longer your life of accountability, the more you'll accomplish.

This means some of your questions will eventually get to the point where they're no longer valid. If you're relying on accountability to get everything in order so you can get into college, once you get that acceptance letter in the mail, you won't need those college-related questions anymore. And that's great! At that point, you can cross that priority off your list and start focusing on other priorities.

Some of your questions may stay relevant for the rest of your life, while others will fall off your list and get replaced by new ones. Either way, you're growing and making progress.

Here's something else to consider: working a little bit ahead of your regular meeting so you can make the most of that time together. In my group, we have an online form that each person spends a few minutes filling out the night before, on their own time. It just contains the questions and a blank space where everyone can type out their answers. Those are then emailed to everyone else in the group so we can all take one another's temperature, so to speak, before we all call in for our weekly meeting. This helps us all get on the same page so we already know what work needs to be done when we get on the line.

Once we start our meeting, the person in charge that week goes around and asks everyone what's going on. If someone has taken a step backward in their struggles, we can ask them what happened and how we can help them back up; if they've taken a step forward, we can all applaud and congratulate them on the progress.

Obviously, this setup works well for our group because we're all professionals from different parts of the country, and I run an extensive website, making it easy for me to create a secure online form for all the friends in my accountability group to use. You probably don't have this type of accessibility, and you may not even feel like you need it, but it's just another consideration as you put your group into action.

One more thing: We take turns leading the discussion each week. The way we assign this works really well for the personalities in our group, though it may not for your group (or for your methodology). The last person to log into the conference call each week has to lead the following week. That way, everyone has some incentive to be on time!

Whether or not you use leadership as a punishment (or incentive, I guess), I'd encourage you all to take turns from week to week leading the group. This way, all the responsibility for the group doesn't fall on one person's shoulders but is spread equally—which is what being open is all about. Because everyone in your group is fully committed to it, you can use a rotating leadership schedule with minimal worry or problems.

Now's the time for you to come up with your specific question or questions. What do you want your group asking you from week to week? Write down the question(s).

MEETING QUESTIONS

CHAPTER 10

HOW DO WE KEEP THIS GOING?

The great thing about the deep bonds of trust and relationship that are formed within an accountability setting is that they don't have to stay in that setting. In fact, my recommendation is that you don't keep your relationship strictly on that level, but that you go beyond the weekly meeting.

There's a high likelihood that your accountability group is made up (or will be made up) of people you already know. If that's so, then you probably don't need to be encouraged to spend time with them outside of your regular meeting. Those are more the types of things that adults with careers and families and church picnics have to be encouraged to do.

But if you don't have that kind of friendly relationship, I'd suggest you do just that—and do it intentionally. Within my group, we have an established rule that you must connect with at least one person from the group each week. And the weekly meeting doesn't count. This doesn't mean we go hang out together all the time (which is actually impossible due to the separated nature of our group of guys), but it does mean we take a few minutes here and there throughout the week to talk about whatever's going on in our worlds, to pray together, to connect if we find ourselves in the same city—those types of things.

If you're already seeing one another frequently, then you don't need to make this type of rule. But if you aren't, then it really helps grow your relationship to make time for each other intermittently throughout your week. It also prevents you from compartmentalizing your accountability into a separate part of your lives.

Guys are notorious for this—for keeping everything we do in its own little box and not letting the contents of those two boxes mix. For example, I once met a guy who uses the XXXchurch accountability software, called X3watch. He has it installed on his computer to prevent him from visiting porn sites on the Internet, and when I met him we were both on a plane leaving Las Vegas, where I lived at the time.

Do you know what this guy had been doing while he was in Vegas? Going to casinos and strip clubs! It's true. I promise I'm not making this up. This guy had taken steps at home to actively avoid online porn, but he saw no problem with taking a trip to Vegas and actively seeking out the live version of it. He could hold both of those thoughts in his head and have no confusion whatsoever because he's a guy, and guys are really good at doing that.

This is an extreme example, but you know what I'm talking about. I'm hoping you can learn how to let the strong bonds you forge through accountability spill into your everyday world, making you all the more strengthened as you live out your day-to-day life.

I have a friend whose accountability group takes this idea very, very seriously. Everyone in the group has a desire to live a life free of porn, and that's one of their main areas of struggle. They're all professional athletes, so they travel a lot from place to place and wind up staying in a lot of hotels. Because of this—and because of the types of in-room movie temptations that are so freely available at hotels—they have a strict rule where everyone in the group knows everyone else's itinerary. As soon as someone checks into their room, they have to disconnect the TV, snap a photo of it, then text that photo to other group members so everyone knows that appropriate measures have been taken to minimize temptation. If this photo doesn't arrive shortly after the itinerary says the guy is supposed to check in, he'll get a phone call from one or more people in the group asking what's going on.

Here's another thing the guys in that group do outside of their regular meeting. Occasionally they'll meet for coffee or just to hang out for a bit, and at any moment each of them has the right to perform what they call an "accountability raid." They immediately demand to inspect another group member's phone for anything crazy. They all have permission to look at anything on each other's phones, specifically for the purpose of keeping each other accountable.

Pretty intense, right?

That's because they're serious about it.

I hope you'll get serious about your accountability as well, using the tools we've covered here to get open and stay that way. It really is a great way to live, free of fear and fully satisfied, knowing you're getting honest and getting real.

Because you've gotten accountable.

Blessings on you as you start this incredible lifelong journey. I'm so excited about the road that lies ahead of you and all the obstacles you'll avoid by not trying to go through life on your own.

You're going to do some great things, because you're never too young to start being open.

CONCLUSION:
ONE LAST THING

If you've done all the exercises in this book, you're now not only fully convinced you need accountability, but you've also done all the practical front-end work that being open requires. Fill in the blanks on the following pages, then copy this list and post it where you'll see it regularly as a reminder that you're on the path to being open.

My Goals

My Accountability Partner(s)

Meetings

Day:

Time:

Our Meeting Location(s):

My Question(s):

Check out the See-Through Life DVD Curriculum

Topics in this series include:

- Lesson 1: The Rewards of Being Open
- Lesson 2: The Power of Honesty and Courage
- Lesson 3: The Impact of the Right People
- Lesson 4: For Girls Only/For Guys Only

Learn more and get started at simplyyouthministry.com